The Trails of a Wild Sunflower

The Trails of a Wild Sunflower

An Anthology

Joy Idowu

A deep dive into the inner workings of my mind and the experiences that shaped my being.

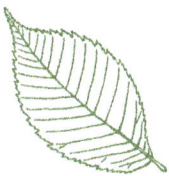

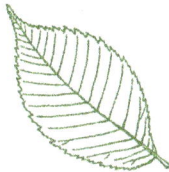

Joy Idowu

Author, Publisher

Instagram: joyandsorrowspoetry

Seth Villamil

Sound Engineer

vitaminseth@gmail.com

Blake Cochlan

Cover Artist

Instagram: pixelatedblake

Portfolio: https://pixelatedblake.myportfolio.com

ISBN (Paperback): 9781739021108

ISBN (E-book):9781739021115

To the girl I once longed to return to-

the wild sunflower that now lives on in my dreams.

Caution

This collection contains mature language, themes of suicidal ideation, and self harm.

Table of Contents

Drowned Out Dreams

Sunflower Field

I dreamed a dream of a sunflower field-

With a little girl frolicking within.

A dream of *joy*.

Peace.

A dream of *life*.

The rain falls, reality sets in.

 It was just a dream.

A memory

Locked away for no evil to find.

What is a dream when you're drowning in the flood
from the endless rain...

Under the storm that causes you pain until your spirit
wanes?

Take me back to the sunflower field.

To the time I could breathe without coughing up
water from my lungs.

I thought rain was supposed to make things new.

A sign that the rainbow will soon shine through.

That's what I was taught.

Now, that idea rots.

I am stuck in the storm with no end in sight.

No energy to fight.

Wishing I could go back to the sunflower field-

Back to *joy*.

Back to *life*.

Down

it's raining down on me.
i can't swim, i'm drowning.

it's raining down on me.
down on me, i can't breathe.

it's raining down on me.
I can't breathe, i'm drowning.

Where It All Began

Three

I was three.

Only three.

Three-year-olds should never have to experience that.

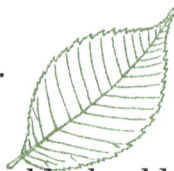

Three years old.

I watched,

Frozen,

As my family stared down the barrel of a gun-

The dark hole that dictated the next minutes of their lives,

Praying to be given a chance to survive.

If they're lucky, a chance to thrive.

That isn't something you forget,

Especially at that age.

Not when you're incapable of grasping what you're a witness to.

The rest of that day is a blur to me now, but that image-

Watching the people I love stare down the barrel of a gun-

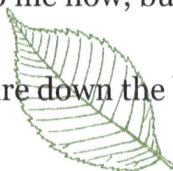

It's vivid, even now.

Fresh in my mind.

It's enough to make a three-year-old livid.

Livid at myself for not doing anything to help.

But really-

What can you do when you're only three?

Logically? Absolutely nothing!

But logic is powerless when your mind is allowed to roam free.

That image-

It was enough to cause nightmares.

Nightmares that lingered as I grew.

Nightmares that made a home out of me before I could even say no.

I was only three, but that didn't matter.

The barrel of a gun doesn't care how old you are-

Neither does life.

Strife is strife,

Even as a three-year-old.

Exodus

If I were given the choice, I would have stayed behind.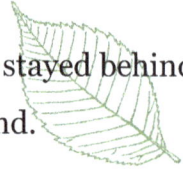

I would have fought to stick with my kind.

Not because it was the smart choice,

It wouldn't even have been the safe choice, but to me–

Eleven-year-old me,

Anything would've been better than moving across the world.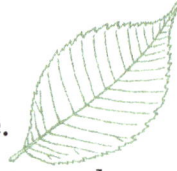

I didn't get to say goodbye.

I didn't get to say goodbye to my home, my friends,

To everything I knew.

Leaving was the best option.

When you're constantly staring down the barrel of a gun–

Knowing it's bound to happen, over-and-over again,

The best you can do is run.

Run far away.

Run across the world.

Run towards the light.

Run towards the opposite of what you were forced to leave behind.

It was the smarter conclusion.

It was the safer decision.

Still, that didn't mean much to me.

Not when it took more than it gave.

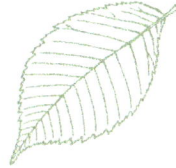

Physically safe was meaningless when mentally, I was at risk.

I was so deep in the red zone that everything I encountered left me thrown.

How safe can you really be-

When you feel like an outsider in your own mind,

Your body, your very own skin?

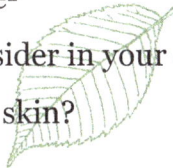

I became so desperate to fit in with anyone that would have me,

Thinking it was the only way to survive.

It's funny what self-preservation can do to a person.

I blame no one for the aftereffects or the permanent defects.

It's the way it all had to be.

It was the beginning of the storm.

The beginning of me drowning in an endless sea.

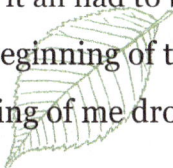

13

Black Don't Crack

We've been called ghetto.

Ratchet.

Some see us as a target,

But that doesn't stop us.

When we say, *"black don't crack"*, that's facts.

We've got it all:

Beautiful ebony skin glowing under the sun,

The culture, the music, mad dance skills.

We're thriving and people try to bring us down.

For what?

Saying *"you act too black"* like that's supposed to be an insult.

I AM BLACK!

That's just a compliment so,

 Thank you.

When that doesn't work, they revert to: "Oh, well, you don't act black."

Is that supposed to mean something to me?

'Cause how am I supposed act? Tell me!

We will not fit into the stereotype you made to
marginalize us.

Pay no attention to the petty "*compliments*" you give
to patronize us.

YOU do not get to define what black is!

Your greedy hands can't touch this.

For so long, you took our land,

Our resources,

Our freedom.

You continue to take, yet you're not satisfied.

You will never be satisfied.

You think we'll let you strip us of our identity?

You think I'll let you strip me of MY identity?

You can spend all your energy trying to degrade us,

Trying to degrade me-

That's just none of my business.

I'll be out here doing my thing-

Styling my hair however I damn well please,

And being *unapologetically black* with ease.

Love and Heartbreak

Love Like This

I have never known,
Nor have I experienced,
A love such as this.
A love so bold,
It would take years to unfold.

A love that rescues.
From stormy nights to sunny days,
From drowning in voids to swimming in daisies.

A love so deep that sacrifice came easy.
Left yourself with no air that I may breathe.
Wounded, so that my scars may heal.
Oh, the honor!

The love you share I don't deserve,
Yet my name is reserved.
Reserved on your heart,
Etched in stone, carved in memory,
Forever and always-

Because those *are* your ways.

You've seen it all.
From the petty lies to the fiends in cages,
The ones locked up for my own safety.
You don't care.
You tell me I have nothing to fear.

You take my hand in yours,
A gesture I feel I do not deserve.
Still, you'd never leave me to rot.

It's madness, in short,
That you still choose love, despite it all.

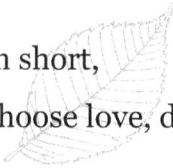

To put it plain and simple,
An attempt, albeit feeble-
I am yours,
And you will *always* be mine.

Say Less

Say less.

Really, say less.

Say nothing at all.

Words leave your mouth like an overflowing river,

Flooding the banks of my mind.

Eroding my roots.

The way you speak…

Constantly.

Flippantly.

With utter disregard for the nutrients that you to deplete.

Albeit unknowingly,

It's exhausting, nonetheless.

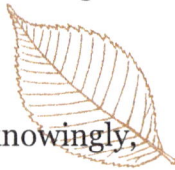

Life and death are in the power of the tongue,

Choose wisely and bear the consequences.

You chose death, yet I'm the one who pays for it.

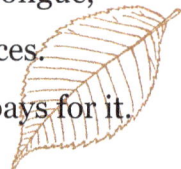

Why am I the one who pays when you continuously speak without thinking?

Just say less.

"I'm sorry. I'll try to think next time. I'm working on it, I promise."

One second later...

You wash away nutrients faster than I can replenish them.

It's never-ending.

Just pause.

Think,

Just for a moment.

Say less,

Or *please* say nothing at all.

Smile For The Camera

Say cheese!

Come on now, smile for the camera!!

Show the world how happy you are!!!

Preserve the moment!!!!

Funny, isn't it?

As a child, you can throw a tantrum.

You are free to cry whenever you're upset.

Cry and you gather an audience.

People pay attention to crying children.

But as an *adult*?

Now you smile for the camera because your feelings don't matter.

Suppress. Depress. All that to impress.

Now smile-

Say cheese to show the world just how happy you are...

"Conceal. Don't feel. Don't let them know."

They don't want to know.

"Don't talk about it. It makes me sad and I'd just rather not."

They don't want to sit with you, try to understand you,

Because it's uncomfortable.

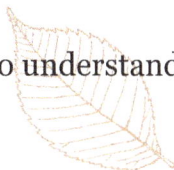

That's not what adulthood is about.

"That's just the way it is". "You're an adult, suck it up". "It is what it is".

NO!

Fuck you!

Maybe I don't want to pretend.

All I've done is pretend for the sake of others.

Now, I'm empty.

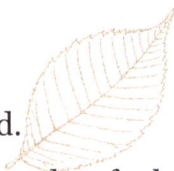

This is how I feel.

This is what's happening to me and there's no "pause" button to hit for your convenience.

So, you know what?

Be uncomfortable.

Look at the camera,

Don't say cheese,

And drop that fake ass smile.

Distant Memory

i thought we were forever

best friends forever

we laughed, and we cried, did everything together

but-

hours turned to days

days turned to months

months into years as you faded away

now all I have left, is a distant memory of you

i told myself not to cry

forced myself to forget

why think of you when you've forgotten me?

tried so hard not to feel, and I called it moving on

who do you turn to when the person you did it all
with-

is nowhere to be found?

time passed

my wounds have scarred

now, you're just a distant memory to me

Goodbye

I refuse to cry over you.

I refuse to acknowledge that what I felt for you was real.

To give you the satisfaction of knowing that you had the power to break me.

But truthfully,

Sometimes I can't help but cry myself to sleep-

Although it's been months.

Although you hurt me.

No one mourns the wicked.

But here I am,

Gutted still.

We should never have happened.

What I saw in you, I will never know-

Maybe it was the attention you gave.

Who doesn't like attention?

You were nice enough, until the end,

But in the end...

You were the tool, and I was the fool.

The fool who cried over you, but I'll never admit that.

Not to your face.

Not because I miss you and not because I ever loved you,

But because you don't deserve it.

I may not be innocent in all this, but at least I know when to quit.

More than I can say about you, but that's where I'll end this story.

Goodbye.

I'm done with you once and for all.

Haunted

There are certain things that are better experienced than read. In my opinion, this chapter is one of them.

Why read about the voices in my head when you can experience a glimpse of what they're like?

This chapter can be experienced in three ways:

-by reading

- by reading with the soundscape.

- by listening to the tracks including the pre-recorded poems in time with the soundscape.

This soundscape is best listened with headphones.

Sing To Me

Sing to me.
Sing to me.

Sing to me a lullaby,
Sing to me a sweet song.
To shut my brain off, fall asleep and float on.

Sing to me for sweetest dreams,
Past the demons and their creed.
Past the storm to the sunshine field-
Where the rainbows and flowers,
They give peace for countless hours.

You know the monsters lurk at night.
They hold max power at witching hour.
I fall prey to their schemes,
Frozen in lucid dreams.

Sing to me so I can sleep,
To ease the urges of pills and heat.

They call out to me; at night they whisper:

"You need my help or else you'll wither.
Only I can give you the peace you desire-
Dear, you already know, I'm not so hard to acquire."

Sing to me a lullaby,
A song for me to go to rest.
Because the demons, they're a pest.
Sing to me for nights on end.

Red Room

Do you hear their screams-
Their cries for help?
They're bottled up.
Each one saved for another day-
The next time you visit.

Welcome to the red room.
All that we do, we do for you.

You cannot escape the *red room*.
Try all you want,
You will always get caught.
Less sleep, more coffee, numbing agents as an aid.
You're fooling yourself.
The red room will come again.

Once you close your eyes, you're in the *red room*.
White lights turn red, in the *red room*.
It is cold yet hot, in the *red room*.
But hey, it is never quiet, never dull, in the *red room*.

Always a new adventure, in the *red room.*

The screams will keep you on your toes.

The mocking laughter of monsters and foes,

Those never get old,

In the red room.

The walls bleed and cry,

You can't stop it all even if you tried.

At least you're never the one in need of saving.

Why be a damsel in distress when you can be a failed hero fading?

Which do you think scars more?

Now that is what the *red room* is for.

You're the special guest in the *red room.*

Everything revolves around you in the *red room.*

We at the *red room* are honored to have you.

Our promise?

It will be a time you never forget.

Witches' Revenge

Something wicked this way comes…

Something wicked this way comes…

Something wicked…

Wicked…

We're back!!

It's witching hour, hunting season.

They're back and out for blood.

They feed on tears and screams and the chaos of it all,

But-

This time, it's not me they want.

Now dear,

Why be a damsel in distress when you can be a failed hero fading?

Why work to break you when you do that-

All. On. Your. Own?

Just the thought of our return knocked you off your throne.

Pathetic.

No better torture than cracking one's mental psyche.

Even better when they do it themselves.

Plant one little seed, a thought, a whisper,

They do your work for you, and they take it much deeper.

They toil the soil that feeds their anguish,

Ensuring witching hour can never vanish.

With no one to blame but themselves,

Now that's the witches' revenge.

Truth is, we only exist within you.

The Hyde to your Jekyll,

Yin and Yang.

You birthed us.

You fed us.

With little to no fuss.

So long as you exist, so shall we.

For richer or poor,

For better or worse,

That's the witches' revenge.

Playground Fun

Goosey-goosey gander, how far I've wandered.

Upstairs and downstairs

Now stuck in hellhound chambers.

On the door, there was a disclaimer.

It read: *"welcome..."* and I stopped there.

Nobody ever reads the fine print.

Hellhounds. Fiends.

They dress to look like friends,

So welcoming in all their affairs,

But their poison, will leave you in tears.

They know how to have fun, I'll admit.

You get lost in their charms, unaware of their little gambits.

I can't help it.

It's hard to resist when they sing:

Ring around the rosie

Ring around the rosie

Ring... Ring... Ring...

Come play with us.

It's been too long.

Haunted

Have you forgotten how much fun we had already?

Your mind is their playground, those bloody hellhounds.

"It's all fun and games."

LIES!

"Don't fuss, no one gets hurt."

YOU do!

You drink and you drink to gain more of their trust,

You're high on their fumes, you forget,

Hellhounds bruise.

So desperate to befriend the ones that hurt you-

Not realizing how much you'll lose when they continue to cut you.

Here's a lesson for you,

One that will always ring true:

Beware who you let in your mind.

You never know what ammo they may find.

They tell you it's all harmless fun, but really,

It's a chase.

You have to run.

Dreamland

Where am I?
What is this place?

It's bright.
Colorful.

The air is fresh, the skies are blue, and it's-

Listen.
Just for a moment.
What do you hear?
I hear nothing.
Absolutely nothing.
It's quiet here.

Peace.
Rest.
No racing thoughts, no shaking hands.
I must be in heaven.
I'm convinced I'm in heaven.

I'm free here.
Weightless.

I made it here! I actually made it!

And look

There's the sunflower field, just like in my dreams-
Maybe a memory?
Over there is the little girl twirling amidst it all.
Her laughter, so light and free.
That's me-
Or what I used to be.

There's music here.
It's soft and sweet.
It's all here like I dreamed.
But this time, it's real!
I'm in heaven!
I made it!

I-

Is that a giant candy cane...? Randomly?

In the middle of the...

Now there's an ice cream pool...

Cotton candy trees, scone bushes, chocolate bunnies

...the yellow brick road?

click *click* *click*

Wake up, it's time for school-

Wake up! Wake up!

WAKE UP!

I'm awake, I'm awake!

Shit...

I'm awake.

Escapism

Caution: This section contains themes of self harm and suicidal ideation.

Euphoria

Feel the blade on your skin,
Erasing all the places you've been.
All the things you've seen.
Fulfilling your need to forget-
To let go.

Starting out is always the hardest step but-
That first taste...
It's enough to leave you wanting more.

Nothing else can make you feel this way.
Nothing else can make you feel so *calm*.
Weightless.

In the moment, the calm is endless.
Watching the scars form, is priceless.
It's a form of bravery,
Knowing you took that first step towards happiness.
Towards true euphoria.

Alas, nothing lasts forever.

The blood dries up.

The scars fade away.

You're back to where you started.

With an itch you can't scratch,

And a hole that isn't easily patched.

Unless...

Unless you do it again-

Again, and again and again.

Instead of endless joy,

You're a slave to a never-ending ploy.

Still hoping.

Praying.

Constantly chasing euphoria,

The chemicals.

You're fueled by paranoia and blinded by a mirage.

Cry, chase, cut.

Repeat.

Welcome to your new life.

I hope it's everything you ever wanted and more.

Fucked

We will never leave.

We will stay and taunt until you rot.

Rent free in your mind.

Forever and always.

We are the voices in your head.

The ones that convince you you're overreacting.

The one that makes you ask:

"Is everything that's happened thus far my fault?"

Child, it *is* your fault.

You were not strong enough.

You let the demons in with open arms.

Doors unlocked, and in we strolled.

"Watch and pray" so you're not prey.

It's too late.

And now-

It's all on you.

You did this to yourself.

Who will love you for what you've become?

Broken souls are the hardest to save-

The hardest to keep.

You can bend over backwards for them,

The ones that say they love you-

But who says you'll end up moving forward?

Now...

Be honest with yourself.

Who really wants you here?

Think long and hard.

It will be easier to disappear than try to act like you're not on the edge.

Sink into the void.

Let the blood drip as you begin to slip.

Match your hands to your heart,

Leave *no* spot unmarked.

Once again, the choice is yours.

This time, we know you'll choose the right one.

Take Your Time With Me

i know you said that you'll always be there, but

sometimes i think that's just too much to bear

i'm telling you

i'm begging you to

take your time with me

i'm a mess of words, mess of feelings

i've been in my head for so long

i'm drowning in this river

please, be patient

i'm still trying to find my way

my way out of this jungle

stay with me

please don't leave me

Let Me Go

Let me go.

You hold on to the memories-

The ones you'll end up forgetting even if I stay.

You hold on to what you hope will be,

What you imagine for me,

That you fail to see-

You hurt me when you hold on too tight.

Holding on because of you causes me to slip further away.

Please let me go.

All things come to an end.

For your sake and mine,

Let me go.

You don't have to agree with me, but please let this end.

Maybe if I continue to hold on, life really will get better.

I know the possibilities that could come if I *"keep keeping on"* but,

I want this to be it for me.

"It gets better."

Maybe, but I'd rather not continue to drag my feet endlessly.

I'd rather not *"walk the walk"* and *"talk the talk"*,

Playing pretend until the void ceases to exist.

Let me rest.

Let me find peace beyond the storm.

I'm blistered and bruised,

Scraped and scratched,

All that and more.

None of which can be fixed with a simple patch.

I know this is selfish.

But maybe this is how it must be.

I saved the most permanent option for last but-

At least you know,

I really did try everything.

Recovery

Wild Sunflower

I dreamed a dream of a sunflower field,

With a little girl frolicking within.

Storms came,

And my dream was out of reach.

I always thought sunflowers and joy were a package deal,

Equated them to how I've always longed to feel.

If sunflowers were joy, then the storms were weeds.

The darkness that continued to feed.

Destroying any sense of life and introducing strife.

Fun fact:

Sunflowers are weeds.

Wild sunflowers.

My idea of joy and happiness,

My idea of everything good in this world-

Is what I equate to everything bad.

Ironic,

In a way that's rather dramatic.

The dichotomy fascinates me, scares me, and
ultimately confuses me.

I've always wanted the calm without the storm,

The rise without the fall.

The gain without all the pain.

Turns out that is the real package deal.

Except,

 Now,

I struggle to accept the pair,

And the space they share.

You cannot have one without the other-

The blue skies and the thunder

That's just the way it must be.

ACKNOWLEDGEMENTS

Special thanks to my friends and family- there are too many to list- for their endless support and encouragement. Self-publishing is a feat and there were times I wanted to give up, but you all, in different ways helped me keep going. Thank you for pushing me to reach my fullest potential, for not giving up on me, and for helping me make this dream a reality. I appreciate you more than you know.

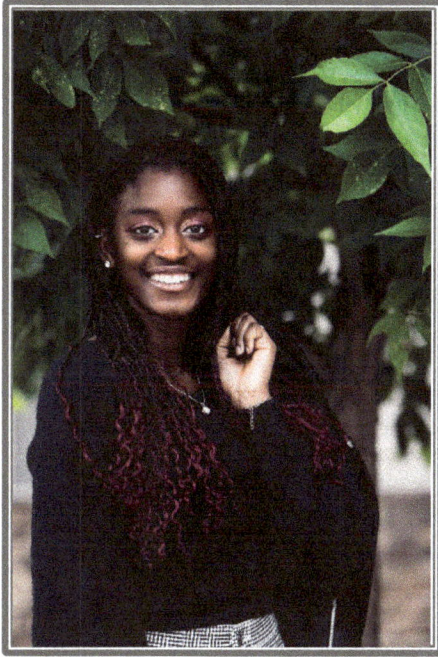

Joy Idowu

Joy Idowu is a Nigerian-Canadian poet based in Calgary. After moving to Canada with her family at a young age, she wrote to cope with the effects of culture shock; starting with rants, which were later turned into poems or songs. This is her first published collection. Outside of writing, Joy is also trained vocalist and chemist.

Photographer: James Idowu

E-mail: jamesidowu113@gmail.com

www.ingramcontent.com/pod-product-compliance
Lightning Source LLC
Chambersburg PA
CBHW071355090426
42738CB00012B/3124